A2 Physical Education
UNIT 6(A&C)

Edexcel

Section A: Exercise & Energy Systems
Section C: Synoptic Analysis

Philip Allan Updates
Market Place
Deddington
Oxfordshire
OX15 0SE

tel: 01869 338652
fax: 01869 337590
e-mail: sales@philipallan.co.uk
www.philipallan.co.uk

ISBN-13: 978-1-84489-014-9
ISBN-10: 1-84489-014-7

This Guide has been written specifically to support students preparing for the Edexcel A2 Physical Education Unit 6 examination. The content has been neither approved nor endorsed by Edexcel and remains the sole responsibility of the author.

Printed by MPG Books, Bodmin

Environmental information
The paper on which this title is printed is sourced from managed, sustainable forests.

Contents

Introduction

■ ■ ■

Content Guidance

■ ■ ■

Questions and Answers

Introduction

About this guide

This guide is written to help you prepare for the Edexcel A2 Physical Education Unit 6 examination, which examines the area of **scientific principles of exercise and performance**. The specification and unit test are split into three sections. Section A covers the concepts of exercise and energy systems. Section B comprises two options: option A is sports mechanics; option B is sports psychology. Section B is covered in another A2 guide. Section C is the synoptic element of Unit 6. It requires you to answer essay questions, making points from both the AS and A2 courses.

This **Introduction** provides guidance on revision, together with advice on how to approach the unit test.

The **Content Guidance** section gives a point-by-point description of all the facts you need to know and concepts you need to understand for Unit 6. Although each fact and concept is explained where necessary, you must be prepared to use other resources in your preparation.

The **Questions and Answers** section shows you the sort of questions you can expect in the unit test. It would be impossible to give examples of every kind of question in one book, but these should give you a flavour of what to expect. Each question has been attempted by two candidates, Candidate A and Candidate B. Their answers, along with the examiner's comments, should help you to see what you need to do to score a high mark — and how you can easily *not* score a mark even though you probably understand the subject of physical education.

What can I assume about the guide?

You can assume that:
- the topics described in the Content Guidance section correspond to those in the specification
- the basic facts you need to know are stated clearly
- the major concepts you need to understand are explained
- the questions at the end of the guide are similar in style to those that will appear in the unit examination
- the answers supplied are genuine answers — not concocted by the author
- the standard of marking is broadly equivalent to that which will be applied to your unit test answers

What can I *not* assume about the guide?

You must *not* assume that:
- every last detail has been covered

- the diagrams used will be the same as those used in the unit test
- the way in which the concepts are explained is the only way in which they can be presented in an examination
- the range of question types presented is exhaustive (examiners are always thinking of new ways to test a topic)

So how should I use this guide?

This guide lends itself to a number of uses throughout your physical education course — it is not *just* a revision aid. Because the Content Guidance is laid out in sections that correspond to those of the specification for Sections A and C of Unit 6, you can use it:

- to check that your notes cover the material required by the specification
- to identify strengths and weaknesses
- as a reference for homework and internal tests
- during your revision to prepare 'bite-sized' chunks of related material, rather than being faced with a file full of notes

The Questions and Answers section can be used to:

- identify the terms used by examiners in questions and what these expect of you
- familiarise yourself with the style of questions you can expect
- identify the ways in which marks are lost as well as the ways in which they are gained

Preparing for the Unit 6 test

Preparation for examinations is a very personal thing. Different people prepare, equally successfully, in different ways. The key is being totally honest about what actually *works* for *you*. This is *not* necessarily the same as the style you would like to adopt. It is no use preparing to a background of loud music if this distracts you. Taking a sporting analogy, the practice environment should mirror the competitive one. The competitive environment is the examination room.

Whatever your style, you must have a revision plan. Sitting down the night before the examination with a file full of notes and a textbook does not constitute an effective plan — it is just desperation! Whatever your personal revision style is, there are a number of strategies you *must* adopt and others you *could* consider.

What you *must* do

- Leave yourself enough time to *cover* all the material identified in the Unit 6 specification.
- Make sure that you actually have all the material to hand (use this book as a basis).
- Identify weaknesses early in your preparation so that you have time to do something about them.

- Familiarise yourself with the terminology used in the examination questions.
- Remember to read though your notes and revision points from Units 2 and 3 of the AS course.

What you *could* do

- Copy selected sections of your notes.
- Summarise your notes into a more compact format, including the key points.
- Create your own flash cards — write key points on postcards (carry them round with you for a quick revise during a coffee break or on the bus).
- Make audio recordings of your notes and/or the key points and play these back.
- Make a PowerPoint presentation of the key points and use this to revise in the last few days before the unit test.
- Discuss a topic with a friend also studying the same course.
- Try to explain a topic to someone *not* following the course.
- Practise examination questions on the topic — particularly planning essay answers.

Approaching the Unit 6 test

Terms used in examination questions

You will be asked precise questions in the examination, so you can save a lot of valuable time — as well as ensuring you score as many marks as possible — by knowing what is expected. Terms most commonly used are explained below.

Brief
This means that only a short statement of the main points is required.

Define
This requires you to state the meaning of a term, without using the term itself.

Describe
This is a request for factual detail about a structure or process, expressed logically and concisely, without explanation.

Discuss
You are required to give a critical account of various viewpoints and arguments on the topic set, drawing attention to their relative importance and significance.

Evaluate
This means that a judgement of evidence and/or arguments is required.

Explain
This means that reasons have to be included in your answer.

Identify

This requires a word, phrase or brief statement to show that you recognise a concept or theory in an item.

List

This requires a sequence of numbered points, one below the other, with no further explanation.

Outline

This means give only the main points, i.e. don't go into detail. Don't be tempted to write more than necessary — this will waste time.

State

A brief, concise answer, without reasons, is required.

Suggest

This means that the question has no fixed answer and a wide range of reasonable responses is acceptable.

What is meant by...?

This usually requires a definition. The amount of information needed is indicated by the mark allocation.

When you finally open the test paper, it can be quite a stressful moment. You may not recognise the diagram or quote used in Question 1. It can be quite demoralising to attempt a question at the start of an examination if you are not feeling very confident about it. However, remember that you have a lot of choice. Read all the questions carefully before deciding which to attempt. Other strategies for the examination itself include the following:

- *Do not* begin to write as soon as you open the paper.
- *Do not* necessarily answer Question 1 first (the examiner did not sequence the questions with your particular favourites in mind).
- *Do* scan *all* the questions on the paper before you start your answers.
- *Do* identify those questions about which you feel most confident.
- *Do* answer *first* those questions about which you feel most confident, regardless of the order in the paper.
- *Do remember* that the essay question in section C scores double and you should, therefore, take more time planning and writing your answer to this part of the paper.
- *Do read* the question carefully — if you are asked to explain, then explain, don't just describe.
- *Do* take notice of the mark allocation and try to match this to the number of points you make in your answer.
- *Do* try to stick to the point in your answer (it is easy to stray into related areas that will not score marks and use up valuable time).

- *Make sure* you fulfil the examination rubric, i.e. answer the correct number of questions from the right sections.

Effective essay writing

The term synoptic refers to an overview of knowledge. In order to answer any synoptic question you should refer to a multitude of topic areas. The main theme for synoptic questions is 'global games' and you will need to refer to a range of examples from various global games in your answer.

The Unit 6 synoptic section has a scientific emphasis.

A good essay will:
- have a clear, recorded plan (which must be flexible and answer the question)
- be at least two sides in length and contain seven or eight paragraphs
- have an introduction that provides an overview of the essay content
- define terms
- work through the question in an identifiable order (e.g. chronologically, with examples in a logical order)
- refer to different global games and not just be a reproduction of an AS Olympic essay
- be analytical and challenge ideas with substantiated argument
- have a conclusion that sums up the answer
- have answered the question

A poor essay will:
- contain the question written out again
- not have a plan
- be written in bullet points
- guess at facts, figures and dates
- have dates out of sequence
- reproduce or regurgitate a premeditated essay plan
- argue a point rather than remaining neutral

In the exam

Read the questions *carefully* — at least twice — to ensure that you understand fully what each question is asking. Plan your time and stick to it. Aim to spend at least 35 minutes writing your essay.

Content
Guidance

This section is a guide to Sections A and C of **Unit 6: Scientific Principles of Exercise and Performance**. The main areas covered are:

- Energy concepts for exercise physiology
- Molecular muscle-cell structures
- Energy systems and the energy continuum
- Physiological adaptations to exercise
- Synoptic topics
  - Individual differences
  - Strategies for training
  - Short-term preparation
  - Long-term preparation
  - The use of technology in sport
  - The use of medicine in sport

You may already be familiar with some of the information in these topic areas. However, it is important that you know and understand this information exactly as described in the specification. This summary of the specification content highlights key points. Therefore, you should find it useful when revising for the Unit 6 test.

content guidance

Energy concepts for exercise physiology

Key points

- Definitions of energy, work and power.
- The different types of energy — chemical, kinetic and potential — how they are measured and the relationship between them.
- How to measure energy output and expenditure.
- The idea of basal metabolic rate (BMR) and the equation that can be used to estimate it.

Introduction

- Energy is defined as the capacity to perform work or put mass into action.
- Work is calculated using the equation:

    work = force × distance

    It can be measured in calories or joules.
- Power is the rate at which work is performed and is calculated using the equation:

    $$\text{power} = \frac{\text{work}}{\text{time}}$$

    It is measured in watts.

In sports science, these concepts are often linked to work out the BMR of an athlete. BMR represents the energy requirements of a person over 24 hours. It is calculated using the following equation:

Women: BMR = 665 + (9.6 × weight in kilos) + (1.8 × height in cm) – (4.7 × age in years)

Men: BMR = 66 + (13.7 × weight in kilos) + (5 × height in cm) – (6.8 × age in years)

Typical figures for BMR are usually given as between 1800 kcal and 3000 kcal per day. However, an active sportsperson training hard may burn up to 7000 kcal per day.

Tip Exam questions often require you to calculate the BMR for given athletes. Practise using the equation and don't forget to take your calculator into the exam.

The different types of energy

The body uses three types of energy:
- chemical
- potential
- kinetic

All energy originates from the sun. Energy enters the body through the first three of the seven food groups. These are:

- carbohydrates
- fats
- protein
- fibre
- vitamins
- minerals
- water

Chemical processes convert the food into glucose, which is used immediately or stored in another form.

The body takes in **chemical energy** in the form of food. This can then be stored as **potential energy** in the form of **adenosine triphosphate** (ATP). ATP is a high-energy phosphate compound, each molecule of which is made up of one molecule of adenosine and three phosphate groups held together by bonds that store the potential energy. Energy from the breakdown of ATP is converted into **kinetic energy** that is used to create movement in the body. This is summarised in the diagram below.

The use of energy in the body

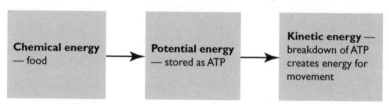

Importance of diet

Diet is very important to athletes. All types of athletes use drinks and foodstuffs to maintain performance through the duration of the activity. These include:

- water and electrolytes
- carbohydrates, both simple and complex
- protein (amino acids)

Athletes seek to fuel contractions at a higher intensity, and for longer, than non-athletes. They may also seek to increase muscle mass. Conversely, athletes in some sports seek to reduce body mass.

What the examiners will expect you to be able to do

- Identify and discuss the concepts of energy, work and power.
- Describe how work and power are calculated and measured.
- Explain the three different types of energy used in the body.
- Explain how energy output and expenditure are measured.

Molecular muscle-cell structures

Motor units and motor neural firing patterns

Key points

- The structure of the motor neurone — you should be able to describe the function of the following components: cell body, dendrites, axon, nodes of Ranvier and myelin sheath.
- The transmission of information at the neuromuscular junction.
- The structure and function of the motor unit and how this is essential for creating the movement required for sport and physical activity.
- An explanation of the all-or-none law.
- Wave summation and the gradation of contraction.

Motor neurones

A **motor neurone** is a nerve cell that conveys nerve impulses from the central nervous system to a skeletal muscle.

A motor neurone consists of three major parts:
- a cell body
- dendrites, which are cellular extensions
- an axon

The structure of a motor neurone is shown in the diagram below.

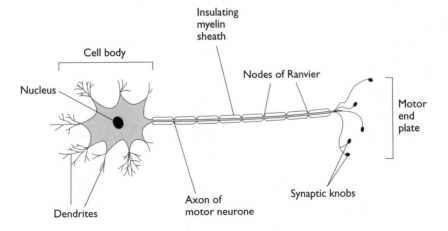

The function and characteristics of the main parts of a motor neurone are summarised in the table below.

Part	Function	Characteristics
Cell body	The centre of operation for the neurone	Found in the thickest region of the cell
Dendrites	Conduct electrical impulses towards the cell body	Branched extensions of the main cell body
Axon	Transmit impulses away from the cell body towards muscle tissue	Surrounded by a myelin sheath that acts as an insulator to speed up the transmission of the impulse
Nodes of Ranvier	Site of the Na^+ gates that allow the nerve impulse to pass along the axon	Spaced constrictions of the myelin sheath
Motor end plate	The junction between the motor nerve and the muscle cell	Also referred to as the neuromuscular junction; a small gap — the synaptic cleft separates the nerve end and muscle cell

Propagation of a nerve impulse

The transmission of a neural impulse along a neurone is an electrochemical process.

For an impulse to be conducted, the neurone has to undergo an **action potential**. This occurs when sufficient numbers of sodium ions (Na^+) have diffused across the membrane into the neurone. (Conversely, when a neurone is not conducting an impulse, it has a **resting potential** brought about by the outward diffusion of potassium ions (K^+) down a concentration gradient.)

Action potentials occur in an '**all-or-none**' fashion. This means that when an action potential occurs, it is always of the same magnitude and duration, no matter how strong the stimulus. During the action potential, the membrane of the neurone is said to be depolarised.

Repolarisation is the return of the membrane potential to the resting potential. The resting potential is restored by the sodium-potassium exchange pump, which returns concentrations to their resting values.

Motor units

A **motor unit** consists of the motor nerve plus the muscle fibres it stimulates. The number of fibres within each motor unit varies according to the precision of the movement required — the larger the movement, the larger the motor unit. For example, one motor unit can stimulate thousands of fibres in a large muscle group — such as the quadriceps when kicking a football.

The sliding filament theory

Key points

- The basic structure of muscle fibres and the relationship between actin and myosin filaments.
- Tracking the breakdown of ATP and its link to the cross-bridges and ratchet mechanism.

Mechanism of muscular contraction

Contraction involves the nervous stimulation of a muscle and the response of the muscle to this stimulation.

It is explained by the sliding filament theory, the stages of which are summarised below:

(1) A nerve impulse arrives at the **neuromuscular junction**, which causes the release of **acetylcholine** from the nerve endings.

(2) Acetylcholine travels across the synaptic gap between the nerve and muscle, stimulating another impulse that travels along the **sarcolemma** (the thin cell membrane).

(3) Small openings inside the sarcolemma carry the impulse through channels called the **sarcoplasmic reticulum**. The impulse passes through to the **myofibril** level (myofibrils are the contractile units of the muscle made up of a series of sarcomeres).

(4) Calcium is stored in the sarcoplasmic reticulum. Once the impulse reaches this site, calcium is released.

(5) The release of calcium allows the cross-bridges on the **myosin filaments** to make contact with the **actin filaments**, allowing ATP to break down and release energy.

(6) The release of energy causes cross-bridge cycling. The actin slides over the myosin, shortening the **sarcomere** and thereby shortening the muscle.

(7) When no nerve impulse is detected, the sarcoplasmic reticulum draws the calcium ions back, preventing the cross-bridges from working and allowing the muscle to relax.

From the diagram below, you can see that the 'A' bands take up the central section of the sarcomere. These bands are made up of thick and thin filaments separated by an 'H' zone. The 'Z' line represents the boundary between one sarcomere and the next. The myosin filaments are the thicker and darker bands; the lighter and thinner actin filaments are found in the 'I' bands, which are at the ends of the sarcomere. These actin filaments also include tropomyosin, a protein that controls muscle contraction by blocking the binding site on the actin filament, which means that the cross-bridges cannot form.

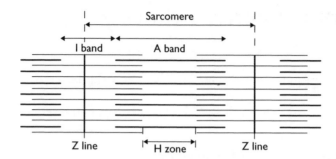

Intensity of muscular contractions

The all-or-none law states that the nerve impulse will not stimulate the muscle fibres until it reaches a certain threshold level. Once the nerve impulse reaches this threshold, all fibres of the motor unit will contract at the same time and maximally. If the impulse is too weak, no fibres will contract at all.

However the intensity of muscular contractions can be changed by varying:
- the number of motor units stimulated
- the frequency at which the impulses arrive at the motor unit

Wave summation

The strength and duration of a muscle contraction can be increased by the frequency of impulses arriving. If a second impulse arrives very quickly after the first stimulus, the time interval between stimuli is not long enough for relaxation of the muscle fibre block to occur and so the tension in the muscle block rises.

Gradation of contraction

Gradation of contraction refers to the ability of muscles to produce forces (tensions) that vary from very light to maximal. This can be achieved by varying:
- the frequency of the stimulus (the number per unit time), which produces contractions of different strengths
- the number of motor units recruited for the activity

This combined effect enables a muscle to exert forces of graded strengths, ranging from fine, delicate, precision-controlled movements to strong, dynamic, powerful movements.

What the examiners will expect you to be able to do

- Describe the structure of the motor unit.
- Explain how a nerve impulse is propagated.
- Explain and track the seven stages of the sliding filament theory.

Tip Visualise a muscular movement that you use in your own sports performance and training, and then try to apply the knowledge about what is happening within the muscle fibres to this movement.

Energy systems and the energy continuum

Adenosine triphosphate (ATP)

Key points

- The role of ATP and its importance in exercise — ATP is the only form of energy the body can use for work.
- The breaking down and resynthesis of ATP.
- The difference between endothermic and exothermic reactions.
- The three energy systems used in sport:
  - ATP–PC (phosphocreatine)
  - lactic acid
  - aerobic
  For each system, you need to be able to comment on the speed of reaction, fuel used, enzyme action, by-products and thresholds.
- How the energy systems are used in different types of exercise to meet energy requirements.

Role of ATP

ATP is a high-energy phosphate compound. Each molecule consists of an adenosine molecule bonded to three phosphate groups. These bonds are high-energy bonds that act as a store of potential energy. When one of these bonds is broken down, energy is released in an **exothermic reaction**. An enzyme called ATPase is required to break down ATP into adenosine diphosphate (ADP), free phosphate and free energy:

$$\text{ATP} \longrightarrow \text{ADP} + P_i + \text{energy}$$

Most energy from the breakdown of ATP is converted into kinetic energy. The remainder is released as heat energy.

ATP can be built up again through a process called resynthesis. Resynthesis of ATP is an **endothermic reaction**, i.e. a reaction that requires energy to work:

$$\text{ADP} + P_i + \text{energy} \longrightarrow \text{ATP}$$

The problem for the sports performer is that muscles have a very limited store of ATP that only lasts for around 2 seconds. In order to supply a continuous source of energy for a longer burst of exercise, ATP has to be resynthesised via the endothermic reaction shown above. The energy required for the resynthesis is supplied via the three energy systems.

Production and resynthesis of ATP

It is important to understand that the three energy systems do not operate in isolation; they interact to supply the energy needed for muscular movement. However, one of the three systems is usually dominant in contributing the energy required for the resynthesis of ATP. The contribution of each energy system is dependent on the intensity and duration of the exercise. This continual interaction between the three energy systems is termed the **energy continuum**.

When the body starts physical activity, it immediately demands an increased oxygen supply to the working muscles. The respiratory and circulatory systems are unable to meet this immediate demand, so the body uses two energy pathways to create ATP **anaerobically** (without oxygen). The two anaerobic pathways produce ATP quickly and powerfully, but they only operate for a short period and give rise to toxic by-products.

If the physical activity is at a reasonable sub-maximal level, then the body is able to produce ATP aerobically because the body's ability to use oxygen can meet the muscles' demands for extra oxygen for greater ATP production. The aerobic pathway has opposite qualities from those of the two anaerobic systems. It can produce ATP for sub-maximal efforts for long periods of time, but cannot produce energy quickly for high-intensity efforts. However, there are no toxic by-products.

The three energy systems used in sport are summarised in the table below:

System	Time of energy provision	Use
ATP–PC (alactic energy pathway)	10–15 seconds of maximal effort	Powerful and explosive activity
Lactic acid	After ATP-PC around 60–120 seconds	High-intensity, sub-maximal activity
Aerobic	After 2 minutes to unlimited	Continuous sub-maximal activities

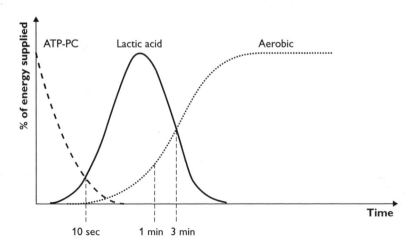

Pyruvic acid is one of the by-products of ATP production. Within the aerobic system, it is broken down via the citric acid cycle and indirectly by the electron-transport chain.

Within the anaerobic systems, the lack of oxygen means that pyruvic acid cannot be processed in this way. It is converted into lactic acid, which forms lactic acid and hydrogen ions.

When lactic acid and hydrogen ions accumulate in the muscles during high-intensity exercise, muscular contractions are inhibited. The body can tolerate increasing levels of lactic acid production only until the lactate accumulation rate is greater than the body's ability to remove it. This is known as the lactate threshold. Once this threshold is passed, performers must reduce or stop their muscular effort.

Optimising performance

In order to optimise the fitness of a performer, training should reflect the specific energy system required. The amount of oxygen consumed gives a good reflection of the energy system used during exercise. By measuring an athlete's oxygen consumption the energy released can be estimated. This is achieved by comparing the oxygen content of the air expelled by the athlete with that of atmospheric air. The maximum amount of oxygen that can be taken in and utilised in 1 minute is referred to as aerobic capacity, or VO_2max.

The ability to work at a high percentage of VO_2max is a good indicator of aerobic capacity. An athlete's aerobic capacity can be improved by sustained periods of aerobic or endurance training.

Tip The 1500 m track race is often used by examiners as a sporting example linked to the energy continuum because it is an event in which all three systems are used by the athletes. Make sure you can identify the pathway used at each stage of the race.

Fatigue and recovery processes

Key points

- The symptoms of fatigue include:
  - depletion of fuels — primarily phosphocreatine (PC) and glycogen
  - an increase in lactic acid
  - dehydration
  - electrolyte loss
- The process of recovery includes the restoration of ATP/PC and glycogen stores, **e**xcess **p**ost-exercise **o**xygen **c**onsumption (EPOC) and a period of oxygen debt.
- How lactic acid is removed and recycled.
- How ergogenic aids can reduce fatigue and speed up the process of recovery.

Fatigue

Fatigue occurs when the body is unable to function at its optimum level because energy levels are depleted. We are most interested in the body's store of **glycogen**. Glycogen is a polysaccharide, consisting of a chain of glucose molecules. It is stored in the muscles and liver and is used as the primary energy source after PC depletion.

Glycogen is used in both the lactic acid and aerobic energy pathways, depending on the intensity of exercise and/or the volume of air available.

During strenuous activity, muscle and liver glycogen is broken down to glucose.

The stages involved are:
- stored ATP — used up
- PC — used up
- muscle glycogen — used up
- liver glycogen — broken down to component glucose molecules that are released into the blood, thus raising the blood sugar levels

When liver glycogen levels begin to run low or are depleted, the resulting low levels of blood sugar produce a feeling of lethargy and fatigue.

Recovery

After strenuous exercise there are four processes that have to be completed before the exhausted muscle can operate at full efficiency again:
- replacement of ATP
- removal of lactic acid
- replenishment of myoglobin with oxygen
- replacement of glycogen

This need for oxygen to replace ATP rapidly and remove lactic acid is known as the **oxygen debt**. More contemporary terms for oxygen debt are **excess post-exercise oxygen consumption** (EPOC) and **oxygen recovery**.

EPOC

Ventilation and heart rates increase during EPOC because:
- lactic acid has to be removed
- ATP has to be replenished
- PC stores have to be replenished
- muscle glycogen stores have to be replenished from lipid stores
- a rise in the temperature of the body means that all reactions are quicker
- respiratory muscles require an increase in oxygen to keep working
- cardiac muscles require an increase in oxygen to keep working
- oxymyoglobin levels need to be replenished

The two major components of oxygen recovery are:
- the fast component — alactacid oxygen debt
- the slow component — lactacid oxygen debt

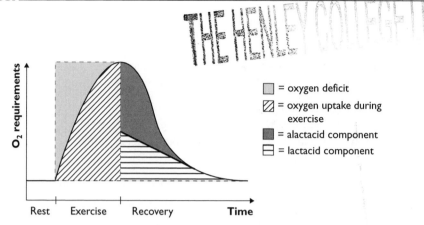

The alactacid recovery phase (fast component) restores the phosphogen stores. Elevated respiration allows the aerobic system to provide energy for ATP and PC restoration. This process requires 2–4 litres of oxygen and takes 2–3 minutes for full recovery.

In the lactacid recovery phase (slow component), most of the lactic acid is converted into pyruvic acid, which is then oxidised via the citric acid cycle, ultimately creating new ATP supplies. Once exercise is finished, the liver can reconvert lactic acid into glycogen. The body removes small amounts of lactic acid through respiration, perspiration and excretion.

The level of exertion determines the level of lactic acid removal. An active recovery or cool down aids this process. This can take several hours and is dependent upon the intensity of the activity and whether the athlete is active or passive during the recovery phase.

Delayed onset muscle soreness

When an athlete suffers muscle pain the day after strenuous activity it is known as **delayed onset muscle soreness** or DOMS.

DOMS results from tissue injury caused by excessive mechanical forces that have been applied to muscle and connective tissue.

The breakdown of muscle proteins causes an inflammatory response that is created as fluid shifts from blood plasma to damaged tissues. This excess fluid then stimulates local pain receptors.

DOMS can be minimised by:
- gradually increasing the intensity of training in order not to overload muscles
- cross training, because aerobic training increases capillarisation within the muscle; this allows greater and faster saturation with blood, which is carrying oxygen and nutrients. This then allows oxygenated blood to reach the lactic acid in muscle cells and therefore the fitter sports person should suffer less from muscle soreness.

Ergogenic aids

An **ergogenic aid** is any factor that enhances performance.

Creatine is an amino acid that is an essential ingredient in the storage of phosphates for the resynthesis of ATP from ADP by the alactic energy pathway.

Many athletes believe that by saturating their bodies with extra creatine for up to 5 days and subsequently taking a maintenance dosage, they will:
- enable prolonged activity fuelled by the alactic energy pathway
- delay lactate accumulation

Other ergogenic aids that athletes sometimes use are summarised in the table below.

Ergogenic aid	Advantages	Status
Anabolic steroids	Stimulate protein synthesis and muscle growth Aid strength training	Illegal
Human growth hormone (HGH)	Stimulates protein synthesis and muscle growth Aids sports with a strength/power focus	Illegal
Amphetamines	Stimulate nervous system and raise arousal levels May reduce feeling of fatigue	Illegal
Caffeine	Stimulates nervous system and raises arousal levels May reduce feeling of fatigue	Legal to a certain limit
Bicarbonate	Acts as a buffer, delaying the fatiguing effects of H^+ lactate in the muscle cells	Legal
Blood doping	Increases the number of blood cells (particularly red blood cells) within the body, which can significantly increase VO_2max	Illegal
EPO (erythropoietin)	Chemical version of blood doping Increases the number of blood cells (particularly red blood cells) within the body, which can significantly increase VO_2max	Illegal

What the examiners will expect you to be able to do

- Identify and discuss how ATP provides energy and how it is resynthesised.
- Compare and contrast the three energy systems the body uses to resynthesise ATP.
- Discuss the notion of the energy continuum and apply it to a range of practical sports examples.
- Identify and discuss why excess post-exercise oxygen consumption (EPOC) occurs after exercise.
- Describe how long it takes to restore energy stores, including phosphocreatine and glycogen.
- Explain the effects of the build up of lactic acid and also how the body removes excess lactic acid.

Tip Put the key terms DOMS, EPOC, EPO, ATP and PC as a message template on your mobile phone. When you have a moment, go through the terms, making sure you can recall their meanings and their roles in the body.

Physiological adaptations to exercise

Key points

- The training effects on energy systems — both short term and long term.
- Physiological adaptations to continuous/aerobic and anaerobic work.
- OBLA (onset of blood lactate accumulation) and DOMS (delayed onset of muscle soreness).

Introduction

There are differences between **responses** to exercise and **adaptations** to exercise:

- Immediate changes that occur to the energy systems during exercise are **responses**.
- More permanent changes as a result of prolonged exposure to a particular type of exercise are **adaptations**.

Knowledge of how the body responds and then adapts to exercise is essential if an athlete is to plan and then monitor an effective training programme.

Responses and adaptations to high-intensity exercise

Responses

Responses to high-intensity exercise include:

- depletion of pre-stored ATP in approximately 2 seconds
- an increase in ADP levels
- increased activity of the enzymes ATPase and creatine kinase, which leads to the breakdown of PC to recreate ATP
- depletion of PC stores in approximately 8–10 seconds
- the start of anaerobic glycolysis after about 5 seconds
- the production of lactic acid
- lactic acid build up, if the intensity is too great
- OBLA if lactate levels reach 4 millimoles per litre
- the possibility of DOMS

Adaptations

Increased efficiency of the anaerobic energy occurs because:

- there is muscle hypertrophy
- there are increased stores of ATP and PC within the muscle cell sarcoplasm
- there are higher levels of enzymes present
- the increased rate of glycolysis results in extended energy production via the alactic energy pathway
- OBLA is delayed
- there is greater tolerance of lactic acid through buffering
- the tendency to experience DOMS is reduced

Responses and adaptations to aerobic exercise

Responses

- The anaerobic energy pathway provides initial energy.
- When an athlete exercises at a constant rate, energy is provided through the metabolism of carbohydrates and fats by the aerobic energy system.
- Carbohydrate stores can support approximately 80 minutes of exercise.
- If the intensity exceeds 60% of VO_2max, then fat cannot be used and energy is created through the breakdown of carbohydrates.
- Higher-intensity exercise uses carbohydrate as an energy source.
- Lower-intensity exercise uses fat as an energy source.

Adaptations

The efficiency of the aerobic energy system, and its ability to sustain activities of prolonged duration, are improved because:

- there is increased capillarisation within the muscles
- there is an increase in both the number and size of mitochondria
- there is an increase in levels of oxidative enzymes, which in turn aids increased aerobic energy production
- levels of stored glycogen, triglycerides and myoglobin are increased
- fat is metabolised more quickly, thus reducing the build up of lactic acid
- there is an increased ability to work at the higher percentages of VO_2max without incurring lactate build up
- the increased size of the heart and strength of muscular contractions increase stroke volume, decrease heart rate and provide a greater scope for work
- cardiac output is increased
- improvements in constriction and dilation of arteries enhances the redistribution of blood, by shunting the supply to the active muscles and tissues
- resting blood pressure is decreased
- number of red blood cells and haemoglobin levels are increased
- the surface area of the alveoli is increased, so pulmonary diffusion becomes more efficient

Lactic acid

Lactic acid is created the moment that exercise begins. If exercise is of low intensity, the body removes lactic acid before it builds up. If exercise is of very high intensity but is short lived, there is insufficient time for lactic acid to build up.

If exercise is of high intensity, lactic acid quickly begins to accumulate. Lactic acid inhibits enzyme production and so eventually will prevent muscular contractions from continuing.

The **lactate threshold** (anaerobic threshold) is a term used to identify the point above which lactic acid begins to accumulate rapidly in the blood of a performer and below which blood levels of lactic acid do not inhibit effort at the desired level. Beyond this threshold, muscle and blood lactate levels increase exponentially and the athlete has to reduce or stop muscular effort. The more accurate term for this point is the **o**nset of **b**lood **l**actate **a**ccumulation (OBLA). If the performer continues to exercise beyond OBLA, although all three energy systems are still functioning, there is an increasing reliance on the lactic acid system. The increasing levels of lactic acid produced further curtail the activity.

Lactic acid is:
- used as an energy substrate and fuels 50% of cardiac contractions
- converted into:
  - carbon dioxide (65%)
  - glycogen and stored in the liver (20%)
  - protein (10%)
  - glucose (5%)

What the examiners will expect you to be able to do

- Understand and to state the differences between responses to exercise and adaptations to exercise.
- Discuss the physiological adaptations to continuous/aerobic work.
- Discuss the physiological adaptations to anaerobic work.
- Explain and apply the concept of OBLA.
- Explain and apply the concept of DOMS.

Tip By the end of this unit you should have concluded your own personal exercise programme. Try to identify any long-term adaptations you have experienced.

Synoptic topics
Individual differences
Key points
- The differences between trained athletes and untrained individuals.
- Issues relating to access and opportunity, including age, gender, race, disability and socioeconomic background.

Links
There are links to the sociocultural issues of access, opportunity and esteem discussed in Units 1 and 4.

Differences between trained athletes and untrained individuals

There are three basic components that differ between trained athletes and untrained individuals:
- physiological — in terms of aerobic and anaerobic training
- psychological — cognitive, psychomotor and affective domains

- mechanical — including the ability to generate and control movement and proficiency in dealing with the effects of outside forces

The benefits of being a trained athlete are summarised in the table below.

Physiological benefits	Psychological benefits	Mechanical benefits
Increase in size, strength and efficiency of the heart, resulting in improved cardiac volume	Responses and actions more consistent	Able to generate effective and efficient movement and understand the underlying science
Increased VO$_2$max and more efficient respiration	Able to produce more efficient, fluent and economic movement patterns	Knowledge of how and when to control stability
Increased energy — both ready-to-use and stored	Able to adapt to differing situations as a result of skills and experience	Able to reduce the negative effects of friction and utilise the positive benefits
Increased tolerance to lactic acid	Able to deal with more demanding competitive situations	Able to move the centre of gravity and understand the underlying science
Delay in reaching the thresholds of the various energy systems	Able to use stress in a positive way to improve performance	Knowledge of how and when to apply spin

Sociocultural factors

The personal circumstances of an individual can affect both access to sport and progression up the sports talent pyramid. The themes of opportunity, provision and esteem were developed in the sociocultural units (Units 1 and 4) and can be applied to an essay answer in this unit.

Opportunity refers to the chance to participate in sport. This is affected by factors such as the availability of time, resources and the fitness and ability of the individual.

Provision relates to where sport can be played. This can be affected by issues such as transport and distance. Elite performers need to be able to train in facilities and venues that are as close as possible to the competitive environment.

Esteem relates to how people feel about their performance in sport. This can affect both access to sport and a performer's confidence. Often stereotypes are associated with esteem. Stereotypes can have both positive and negative effects on performance and participation.

There are five main sociocultural factors that are included under individual differences:

Age
Strength peaks at around 20–30 years. In some sports, such as swimming and gymnastics, the peak age is much lower. However, for most sports the mid-30s appears to be a cut-off point beyond which progression cannot be achieved.

Gender

Males are stronger than females. However, evidence now suggests that women may be more suited than men to endurance events.

Few sports allow women and men to compete equally. There is a link here to race, in that some cultures and religions do not allow women to compete or train.

Race

There is evidence to support the idea that some races are suited to particular sports. However, it is often social factors that dominate, particularly those relating to access and provision. Stereotyping linked to racial groups is manifest in the concepts of stacking and centrality.

Disability

Disabled people are disadvantaged when compared with able-bodied performers. However, the Paralympics and other competitions for the elite disabled are raising profiles. Access to sport is a key issue for the disabled.

Socioeconomic background

For people on low incomes, access to transport, resources and time are the main limiting factors. However, for people in poorer social groups, sport can also be seen as an escape route.

Winning the gender race

Recent research suggests that within 150 years women sprinters may run faster than men. Some scientists argue that if current trends continue, the fastest athlete at the 2156 Olympics may be a woman, ending thousands of years of male physical supremacy.

At the women's first 100 m Olympic final in Amsterdam in 1928, the gold was won with a time of 12.2 seconds — 1.4 seconds longer than the men's race. By 1952, the gap had shrunk to 1.1 seconds. The men's 100 m was won in 10.4 seconds, the women's in 11.5 seconds. In four of the five Olympics from 1988 to 2000, the difference was under a second. If this trend continues women may indeed ultimately catch up with the men.

One reason why female athletes are catching up with men is the recent increase in access to training, sponsorship and events previously only available to men. The women's Olympic 100 m did not start until the 1920s; the women's marathon did not start until 1980.

However, though women do appear to be progressing at a faster rate than men, there are fundamental physiological differences between men and women that are particularly important in sprinting and other events that require muscular power. Success in sprinting depends on power and muscle mass. The male hormone testosterone is important in developing muscle mass and men will always have higher levels of this hormone than women.

In sports that rely on technology that evens out the natural gender differences, greater improvement can be seen. For example, in the pole vault it will come down to the power of the male athletes versus the agility and increased flexibility of the females.

What the examiners will expect you to be able to do

- Identify and explain the differences between untrained people and trained athletes.
- Discuss how individual differences can affect both access to sport and progression through the talent pathway.
- Comment on the five main sociocultural factors that can contribute to individual differences.

Links

Most of the work in this section will have been covered in the skills acquisition section of Unit 2. You should read through your notes from this section as part of your revision.

Strategies for training

Key points

- The role of the leader (coach or manger) in developing performance.
- Cultural variation, including differing societal ethics and values, particularly the win ethic versus the recreational ethic and their influence on sport.

Leadership

There are a number of leadership roles within sport; these leaders play an important part in developing performance.

In order to be successful, effective leaders require thorough knowledge both of their sport and of the factors that affect performance. They need to be able to plan and utilise the different cycles of training — macro, meso and micro. Leaders also need to understand and be able to use a variety of teaching styles. They should be able to adapt these styles to suit the learning phases of their performers and particular situations.

The style and type of leadership can be affected by the cultural setting. Often the prevailing sporting ethic governs the styles of coaching and teaching. There are three main ethics found in sports cultures:

- **Win ethic** — the aim is to win at all costs. This may result in an autocratic approach to coaching. In following this ethic, coaches and performers are driven by results.
- **Radical ethic** — winning is important, as is the style of play and level of performance. Coaches may have a wide knowledge of tactics and strategy and be prepared to be innovative in their approach, which will be more person-oriented.
- **Recreational ethic** (referred to as the counter-culture ethic in the USA) — taking part is the dominant drive. Coaches will be both person-oriented and task-oriented. They may also have a laissez-faire approach to coaching.

What the examiners will expect you to be able to do

- Discuss and debate the role leaders play in developing performance.
- Discuss how a leader's style needs to adapt to suit both cultural needs and the needs of the performer.

Short-term preparation

Key points

- Methods of short-term physiological, psychological and mechanical preparation prior to performance and/or competition.
- Effects of motivation, intrinsic rewards and extrinsic rewards on short-term preparation.
- Importance of pride, passion and nationalism.
- The social factors that affect short-term preparation.

Physiological, psychological and mechanical aspects

Short-term preparation involves the period immediately before a performance. The three aspects of short-term preparation you need to review are:

- physiological
- psychological
- mechanical

Short-term preparation can also be affected by social factors, particularly the influence of intrinsic and extrinsic rewards and of pride and passion.

Physiological aspects

Aspect	Action
Tapering training	Reducing the intensity and duration of training as competition approaches to ensure that energy stores are as high as possible
Acclimatisation	Adapting or adjusting to the specific environment expected during the competition
	May involve selecting equipment, footwear and kit to suit the competitive environment
Adapting nutrition	May involve carbohydrate and creatine loading to maximise stores
	Increasing fluid intake before competition to reduce risk of dehydration
Thorough warm-up	Pulse-raisers followed by flexibility and skill-based activities

Psychological aspects

Aspect	Action
Motivation	Discussing the influence of extrinsic and intrinsic factors
	Setting goals for individuals, teams and squads
Developing a positive attitude	Focused and selective attention
	Working through game plans and strategy
	May include watching videos of the opposition and/or watching own successful performances
Dealing with anxiety	Recognising the symptoms of anxiety and stress — especially somatic symptoms
	Using anxiety in a positive manner

Aspect	Action
Psyching-up — arousal	Understanding the inverted U-theory and applying it to individuals and teams
	Knowledge of psyching-up and psyching-down
	Use of ergogenic aids (e.g. music) to help performers reach the optimum zone

Mechanical aspects

Aspect	Action
Playing surface	Affects choice of footwear — may need to increase or reduce friction
	Development of fast tracks and pools
Kit and equipment	May need to adapt to environmental and climatic changes
	Wearing specialist equipment for improved performance and health and safety
Techniques and strategies	Adaptation of techniques and strategies to suit the opposition and the environment, for example applying spin to balls and changing the speed of release
	Other factors to counter the opponents' strengths

Social factors that influence short-term preparation

Global games are very important in terms of national pride and the chance for a country to gain shop-window success. In some ways, sporting competition has replaced the wars that, before the industrial revolution, countries used to fight in order to gain supremacy.

At all global games there is formal recognition of national identity. This usually involves playing the national anthem or, in the case of the Olympics, marching into the stadium behind a national flag. This has an effect on athletes' short-term preparation, particularly in terms of arousal and mental preparation for competition.

Sport has been used to allow countries to develop national identities. This is especially true among nations with short histories such as Australia and the former East Germany. It is also a vehicle for developing and emergent cultures to gain recognition. For example, Kenya and Ethiopia are now globally recognised as world powers in middle-distance and long-distance running.

Before major global games, the media often 'hype up' big matches. This is particularly true of European soccer championships. Often, war-like terms are used in the description of coming fixtures, especially between old enemies such as England and Germany. This can affect the mental preparation of both performers and spectators.

Some teams also make reference to traditional culture in their short-term preparation. The New Zealand rugby team always perform a 'haka' — a traditional Maori war dance — before each game. This acknowledges the traditions of the country and can be closely linked to the theories of inverted-U and selective attention that you might have covered in the sports psychology option.

What the examiners will expect you to be able to do

- Discuss the effects of motivation, intrinsic rewards and extrinsic rewards on preparation for sports competition.
- Highlight the main considerations that should be included in a performer's short-term preparation.

Long-term preparation

Key points

- Physiological, psychological and mechanical aspects of long-term preparation prior to performance and competition.
- Support roles, finance and administration involved in preparing elite athletes — in particular, the use of academies and institutes.
- Cultural differences in the preparation and nurturing of elite athletes.

Physiological, psychological and mechanical aspects

Physiological aspects

Physiological aspects of long-term preparation include:
- identifying needs — gap analysis and testing
- specific fitness training
- meso- and macro-cycles of training
- principles of training
- nutrition — carbohydrate loading
- ergogenic aids — training aids and supplements

The key word here is adaptation. Consistent training for a period of at least 6 weeks should bring about long-term physiological changes.

Psychological aspects

Psychological aspects of long-term preparation include:
- identifying needs
- goal setting — SMARTER
- skills development
- imagery
- coping strategies

content guidance

- team development
- leadership

Mechanical aspects

Mechanical aspects of long-term preparation include:

- development of technique, through the use of video and biomechanical analysis
- the use of ergogenic aids to improve performance
- improving and adapting training equipment to mirror the competitive environment
- adapting and modifying clothing and footwear to reduce the effects of drag and friction

Supporting elite athletes

In the run up to the 1936 Berlin Olympics, Hitler had pioneered an approach using training camps and coaching in an attempt to ensure Aryan supremacy at the games. After the Second World War, the Eastern bloc countries were the first to develop a systematic approach to nurturing elite sports talent.

The Eastern bloc approach

The Eastern bloc approach focused on the identification of talent in young children — often as early as primary school. This was followed by full-time specialist training by professional coaches, which was funded by state governments. In the final phase of preparation, the best athletes would live and train at specialist centres (institutes) of sports excellence. The system was extremely successful, though recent revelations of widespread drug abuse has somewhat tarnished this model of nurturing talent.

Western cultures

In western cultures, the historical divide between amateurism and professionalism delayed any sustained approach to elite sports development. For most of the twentieth century, Olympic sports had to rely on the voluntary sector raising money through donations and fundraising events. Schools and universities took the central role in identifying and developing talented sports performers.

By the 1970s, the rise both in playing standards and in rewards (political and financial) available in global sport led to all cultures reassessing their approach to supporting elite performers. France became the first western culture to adopt an Eastern bloc-type centralised approach to elite sport by setting up a National Sports Institute (INSEP). Australia quickly followed, establishing the AIS in 1981.

North America

In North America, an alternative system of nurturing sports talent emerged, based around the college scholarship system. This enabled performers to train full-time, using the excellent sports facilities offered by all colleges, and to receive athletic scholarships so that their amateur status was not affected.

Resulting models of nurturing talent

By the 1980s, there were two main models for nurturing talent:
- a centralised model in which athletes received state scholarships
- a USA-style university model in which athletes received athletic scholarships

Both of these models were given the label 'shamateurism', as they abused the concept of an amateur athlete.

The UK has relied heavily upon the voluntary sector to support and finance its elite athletes. The UK is now unique in that most of its Olympic athletes receive no direct funding from the government. Before the change in the rules regarding amateur status, the Sports Aid Foundation provided most of the limited grants available for elite athletes in the UK. Since the end of the 1990s, this role has been taken on by the national lottery through the sports lottery fund, which is distributed by UK Sport.

Most cultures have now adopted a centralised approach to sports excellence based around national centres of excellence. The benefits of such an approach include:
- bringing together the best coaches
- making available the best possible facilities
- allowing performers to concentrate on full-time training
- creating an atmosphere of excellence
- allowing the transfer of knowledge as well as skills and training methods between different sports
- being a more efficient method of directing funds
- being more effective, in large countries, in bringing elite sports squads together in one place

Funding elite athletes

The funding of the preparation of elite athletes differs according to the nationality and cultural background of performers and teams. The following points should be considered:
- the use of state sponsorship and the political ties this may create — this approach was first used by East Germany and the Soviet Union
- the use of academic scholarships to help students and young people train in their specific sports — this approach has been used successfully in North America for the past few decades
- private–sector sponsorship and endorsement of elite performers — this only occurs in a small number of sports and with particular performers that are 'telegenic'
- the professional sports scene in a particular culture
- the financial contributions made by national lotteries and voluntary sectors — this is the main source of funding for Olympic preparation in France and the UK

What the examiners will expect you to be able to do

- Highlight the physiological, psychological and mechanical factors that should be included in a performer's long-term preparation.
- Discuss the support roles, finance and administration involved in preparing elite athletes and how these differ amongst cultures.

The use of technology in sport

Key points

- The role of technology in training analysis, and in enhancement and evaluation of sporting performance.
- The concept of sports science and support and the roles they now play in preparing performers for global sports competitions.
- The influence of the media on sporting performance.
- The influence of the media on sports performance, assessment and reward.

Technology in the preparation of athletes

Technology can be applied to three main areas of athlete preparation:
- training analysis
- enhancement of performance
- evaluation of performance

Performers can undertake **internal monitoring**. The most commonly used techniques are recording and analysing heart rate and blood lactate levels. These data can be used to determine when an athlete is moving between energy systems.

External monitoring includes video analysis, force measurement, muscle activity assessment (electromyography) and photography. These can be used to adapt techniques and skills in order to improve performance.

Ergogenic aids can be applied to the following areas of preparation:
- drugs and supplements
- clothing
- equipment
- training simulators
- fitness equipment

Recent examples of technology used in elite sport include hypoxic training and alba machines:
- **Hypoxic training** involves training or sleeping in a room or tent in which the oxygen content has been reduced from 21% to 15%. These low oxygen levels encourage the kidneys to produce more erythropoietin (EPO), which results in the production of more red blood cells. This helps maintain peak fitness and helps accelerate healing of damaged tissue.
- **Alba machines** are used in the rehabilitation of injured athletes. Computer technology pinpoints an injury and heats the affected area to 40°C. This increased temperature stimulates blood flow up to a rate 15 times faster than normal and leads to a more rapid rate of healing.

Genetic engineering

Research into the genetic code of humans has created the possibility of major advances in the treatment and prevention of many serious diseases. However, this positive medical breakthrough raises the question of abuse by sports performers.

Research and debate among sports scientists, particularly Munthe (2000), have identified ways in which genetic engineering could be abused in sport, including:

- making it possible to fine tune the chemical composition of a drug to suit better the genetic make-up of an athlete or using the knowledge of an athlete's genetic make-up to optimise training and nutrition programmes
- applying gene technology to modify red blood cells or the production and release of various sports-related hormones — this could include stimulating the body to release greater amounts of natural EPO
- using genetic knowledge to create modifications very early in the life of human beings — or even in the fertilisation of eggs — in order to create 'bionic' athletes
- using genetic data to select individuals for sport — young athletes whose genetic make-up suggests that they are unlikely to reach the highest levels of performance could be identified before a governing body or sponsor invested too much money in them

Although both the World Anti-Doping Agency and the IOC have considered the implications of advances in genetic modification for their joint world anti-doping code, there are currently no clear rules or punishments that deal specifically with the concept of genetic engineering within sport.

The influence of the media on sporting performance

In the twenty-first century, the media have a huge influence on global sport in terms of both funding and promotion, as well as providing a stage for nations, groups and individuals to perform and gain recognition.

A number of key influences could be discussed:

- The media provide a forum for opinion and debate.
- The media influence the nature and scale of financial reward.
- Individuals and nations are provided with a stage on which to perform and/or protest.
- Sports stars are turned into celebrities. This brings increased financial rewards but also opens up their private lives to public view.

What the examiners will expect you to be able to do

- Explain the role of technology in training analysis and evaluation.
- Discuss the concept of sports science and other support and the role they now play in preparing performers for global sports competitions.
- Discuss the influence of the media on sports performance, assessment and reward.

Tip Keep an eye on the sporting news. In the synoptic essay, you score higher marks for originality, so try and use up-to-date contemporary sporting examples in your answer.

The use of medicine in sport

Key points

- Sports medicine and its use in the development of sports performance.
- The link between nutrition and performance.
- The legal and illegal use of drugs in sport.
- Ethics and pressures relating to drug abuse.

Nutrition and preparation

A balanced diet, especially in relation to complex carbohydrates, is important.

Adjustment of diet before competition might include:

- carbohydrate loading (carbo-loading) to ensure maximum storage for performance
- creatine loading

A diet high in carbohydrates ensures that the glycogen stores in the body are as full as possible. In order to carbo-load, an athlete's diet must contain 70% complex carbohydrates. Modern thinking suggests that all athletes should maintain full-time carbo-loading.

Creatine monohydrate is a key supplement used by many elite athletes. It increases PC stores in the body and therefore causes a rise in the threshold of the alactic system. Creatine loading specifically aids sports where work is intermittent. The additional creatine improves recovery time and allows athletes to train at a higher intensity for longer.

The importance of hydration

It is suggested that a 1% drop in the hydration level of an athlete can lead to a 10% reduction in performance. Therefore, it is very important for athletes to manage their fluid intake carefully. **Dehydration**, which is a result of excessive water loss, also results in loss of salt and calcium.

Links
This links to short-term preparation for global competition.

Dehydration during competition can lead to cramp and loss of muscle efficiency. This can be witnessed at the end of competition, particularly when games such as football and rugby go into extra time.

As more water is lost, the volume of plasma decreases and the concentration of the remaining salt increases.

Dehydration has a negative effect on performance because:

- it leads to a decrease in blood volume
- it leads to a decrease in tissue fluid formation

- it leads to an increased heart rate
- the body retains more heat

The best way of preventing dehydration during competition is regularly to drink small amounts of water or a glucose drink before and, where possible, during the competition. It is also wise for athletes to stay away from caffeine drinks and alcohol in the period before competition because these have a diuretic effect on the body.

The use of drugs in sport

In sport, a drug is classed as a substance that can be taken in a variety of ways to produce physical or psychological advantages for the person taking it. What is sometimes overlooked is the fact that drugs may also cause some unpleasant and unwanted side effects.

Drugs in sport are those chemicals and substances that are on the banned (red) list issued annually by the IOC's Medial Commission. Other chemicals, which are not on this list, are referred to as supplements. These are legal and athletes are free to use them in their preparation and training. However, there is often a fine line between what is classed as a drug and what is classed as a supplement.

Some sportspeople decide to take drugs to enhance or improve their performance or are encouraged to do so by their coach. The temptation is great because the stakes are so high. Winning a gold medal at the Olympics can be worth millions of pounds in sponsorship and endorsement deals.

Links
This issue can be linked to the increasing dominance of the win ethic in global sport.

The use of drugs continues to increase in sport and the technology is becoming more sophisticated. Examples of this development include blood doping and the use of EPO.

Blood doping
Blood doping is a method of increasing the number of red blood cells in the body. This means that more oxygen is carried to the muscles. It is most often used by athletes who compete in high endurance races, such as cycling or cross-country skiing.

In the past, a litre of blood would be removed from an athlete's bloodstream and then frozen and stored for several weeks. A day or two before a big race, the stored blood would be re-injected into the athlete's system, adding extra red blood cells. These extra red blood cells would carry more oxygen to the muscles, giving the athlete an advantage over other racers who did not use blood doping.

EPO
Generally, athletes no longer re-inject blood. Instead, cheating athletes inject genetically engineered drugs that cause the body to create extra red blood cells. EPO is the most commonly used blood doping chemical. It is a drug that is used to treat patients with kidney disease.

EPO was made famous by the Festina cycling team during the 1998 Tour de France cycle race. The Festina team was expelled from the race after the car belonging to the team masseur was found to contain a large quantity of EPO. If it had not been for the discovery of the drug in the car, the athletes could have continued taking it. They would not have been found out because there was no reliable test for EPO available in 1998.

Drugs and sporting ethics

The main concerns over drug taking in sport are based on the following ethical issues:

- Athletes may suffer physical or psychological harm as a result of drug use.
- The use of drugs by one athlete may force other athletes to take drugs in order to maintain parity.
- The use of drugs in sport is unnatural. Any resulting success is due to external factors and therefore the performer fails to achieve the intrinsic rewards. This is often referred to as the 'hollow victory'.
- Athletes who use drugs gain unfair advantage over athletes who do not use them.

Cover-up and scandal

The Sydney Olympic Games of 2000, although managing to stay largely drug-free during the competition, have been linked to attempts to cover up drug use by elite athletes from a number of nations. Most shocking is the evidence that the USA Track and Field Federation (USATF) are alleged to have covered up ten positive drug tests. Rumours of drug cover-ups have existed for as long as testing for drugs has existed, but until now, confirmation of these rumours has never been made public. In the light of these discoveries, the USATF has promised to crack down on drug use and take a harder stance against those athletes who test positive.

Tackling the cheats

The World Anti-Doping Agency (WADA) was established in November 1999 and charged with promoting and coordinating the fight against doping in sport. WADA is governed by a board that includes representatives from the major international sporting organisations, including the IOC, as well as sports ministers from a number of governments. So far, its primary aim has been to fund a considerable increase in the annual number of drug tests and to produce a world anti-doping code. The main focus of this code is to regain athletes' confidence in doping control policy and to develop a framework that is consistent in its application, effective in its management and which respects and promotes the rights of athletes.

What the examiners will expect you to be able to do

- Outline issues in sports medicine that relate to the preparation of athletes.
- Explain the link between nutrition and performance.
- Discuss the use of drugs in sport, to include legal and illegal usage.

Tip Keep your eyes on the sporting news. In the synoptic essay, you score higher marks for originality, so try to use up-to-date, contemporary sporting examples in your answer.

Questions
&
Answers

This section contains questions similar in style to those you can expect to see in your Unit 6 examination. The limited number of example questions means that it is impossible to cover all the topics and all the question styles, but they should give you a flavour of what to expect. The responses that are shown are real students' answers to the questions.

There are several ways of using this section:

- 'Hide' the answers to each question and try the question yourself. It needn't be a memory test — use your notes to see if you can actually make all the points you ought to make.
- Check your answers against the candidates' responses and make an estimate of the likely standard of your response to each question.
- Check your answers against the examiner's comments to see if you can appreciate where you might have lost marks.
- Check your answers against the terms used in the question — did you *explain* when you were asked to, or did you merely *describe*?

Examiner's comments

All the candidate responses are followed by examiner's comments. These are preceded by the icon *e* and indicate where credit is due. In the weaker answers, they also point out areas for improvement, specific problems and common errors, such as lack of clarity, weak or non-existent development, irrelevance, misinterpretation of the question and mistaken meanings of terms.

Training and testing for aerobic capacity

In preparing for a major competition, elite performers train with the aim of enhancing their aerobic capacity.

Using specific examples, describe how you would plan and test a training programme that could be used to enhance an athlete's aerobic capacity.

What factors have to be taken into account when carrying out tests and training programmes?

(11 marks)

Total: 11 marks

■ ■ ■

Candidates' answers to Question 1

Candidate A

If I were to test and plan a training programme to enhance an athlete's aerobic capacity there are a number of things that I would need to take into account. First, I would use a fitness test such as the multi-stage fitness test to identify the existing level of performance. I would then be able to find the intensity at which the athlete would need to perform in order to improve. I would then identify the stage in the athlete's competitive season to ensure that the training plan would not interfere with long-term goals.

I would then work with the athlete to agree on macro-, meso- and micro-cycles. The training would involve mainly sub-maximal exercise such as swimming, jogging and cycling sessions, in both fartlek and continuous modes. This would ensure that maximum improvement is achieved. After 5 weeks, which would represent the meso-cycle, I would monitor progress by re-testing the athlete using the multi-stage fitness test. This would allow evaluation of the progress made up to that point. I would also evaluate each of the individual sessions for intensity using the Borg scale. In addition I would monitor nutrition, hydration and how the athlete feels after each training session. This would give an indication of the success and relevance of the sessions, so that they could be adapted accordingly.

Factors such as the athlete's position in the season (e.g. pre-, mid- or off-season) need to be considered to ensure that the athlete is not overloaded prior to competition. Health and well-being are also important in order to avoid injury and fatigue.

I would have to ensure that testing was carried out when it would not affect the athlete's performance in competition. It should be done at a point in the programme at which improvement is expected.

Using the macro (season), meso (4–6 weeks) and micro (1 week) theory of planning, I would identify goals for the athlete. By testing, I would recognise whether these goals were realistic. For example, if a goal of 10% improvement in aerobic capacity after 5 weeks proved to be unrealistic, then it could be changed.

Candidate B

Test

The test could be a multi-stage fitness test. This would be relevant for aerobic capacity because the performance has to be carried out for over 60 seconds.

Training

The training method could be jogging — continuous at a low intensity and then slowly increasing the intensity, so that the performer works at a high intensity to measure cardiovascular fitness.

The performance would have to be at a high intensity (about 17+ on the Borg scale) so the lactic acid energy system will be used. The performer will go into oxygen debt and have to stop while the oxygen debt is repaid.

The test score on the multi-stage fitness test will show the level the performer achieves. Using tables, this score can be converted to give the athlete a predicted aerobic capacity or VO$_2$max.

Factors

When carrying out the test and training, many factors have to be taken into account. If performers overtrain, they may suffer fatigue. This is muscular tiredness that prevents performers from maintaining maximum energy output. This may well become evident in the test of aerobic capacity, as training should be carried out at least 3–4 times a week. Also, training sessions and tests may have to be adjusted if the athlete receives an injury. The final point is that to be successful in their training, athletes should adapt their diets, for example they should include complex carbohydrates for energy.

e This question requires candidates to work through a number of stages. It is a type of question that requires some planning. Using headings from the question can help with the structure of the answer, and Candidate B uses this technique well. Candidate A sets out a thorough answer and manages to answer all parts of the question. The answer provides good detail and links in the facts about periodisation well. The factors that could affect testing and training are clearly set out. Candidate B also manages to answer all parts of the question, but not with the same level of detail. Many of the points towards the end are brief and need more explanation. Candidate A scores 9 out of the possible 11 marks, while Candidate B scores 7.

Dehydration and athletic performance

Dehydration is a problem that can seriously affect the performance of endurance athletes.

What steps can an athlete take to avoid dehydration on the day of competition? (4 marks)

Total: 4 marks

■ ■ ■

Candidates' answers to Question 2

Candidate A

Athletes can ensure that before competition they consume the recommended amount of water (around 4 litres) and that they increase the level of hydration if the intensity of training increases. As they prepare for the start of competition they need to take regular drinks to ensure that they are fully hydrated. However, they should avoid drinks that are high in sugar because these would affect blood sugar levels and, therefore, the release of energy. They must ensure that during the competition they make use of opportunities to rehydrate, by taking on small amounts of fluid regularly. Some sports allow this and give players breaks for drinks. In sports that do not, it is important that drinks bottles are left around the arena. Isotonic drinks may be the best for rehydrating because they contain sodium and potassium. After competition, athletes should drink plenty of fluids to replace the fluids lost during competition.

Candidate B

Dehydration should be avoided by an athlete. The performers should have plenty of fluid in their diets but should not overdo it before a competition. The performers should be able to receive fluid through different sources.

🖉 Both candidates appear to have a grasp of this common exam topic. Candidate A clearly answers the question set and gives good detail regarding the build-up to a competition. Candidate A backs up points well, giving practical examples as well as figures and facts and scores the maximum 4 marks. Candidate B only gives a brief overview and does not make enough points to match the marks available and scores only 1.

uestion **3**

Carbohydrate loading

What is 'carbo-loading' and what type of sports performer would benefit from this nutritional practice? Relate this to a training programme.

(4 marks)

Total: 4 marks

■ ■ ■

Candidates' answers to Question 3

Candidate A

Carbo-loading is a process whereby, 2–3 days before competition, athletes no longer take in much carbohydrate — instead they eat more protein and fat. Then, 24 hours before competition they consume an increased amount of complex carbohydrates, such as pasta, rice and potatoes. This process allows the athletes to store more carbo-hydrate than usual. This is most beneficial to athletes involved in long-distance events such as marathons. However, this practice needs to be thought about during the training programme, because a reduction in energy stores during the carbohydrate starvation period could mean that athletes struggle to train effectively. The training programme would have to be adapted, for example by reducing the intensity of training during this stage.

Candidate B

Carbo-loading is when an athlete has carbohydrates before a performance. This is very common in sport today. Carbohydrate is the optimum store of energy the body can use during sport. Carbo-loading is used to enhance performance because it maximises the store of carbohydrates in the body. It is achieved by eating large amounts of complex carbohydrates a few days before competition.

🖉 Both candidates give a sound definition of the term carbo-loading, which answers the first part of the question. There is a contrast in the number of points made by the candidates and this links to the marks awarded. Candidate A makes more than four valid points and scores the maximum 4 marks. Candidate B only makes three points and does not give an example of a sport that would benefit from carbohydrate loading or relate to a training programme. Therefore, the candidate does not answer the question fully and only scores 2 marks.

Question 4

Lactic acid

During high-intensity exercise, there is an increase in the level of lactic acid. State the physiological effects that this increase has on a working muscle and comment on the fate of lactic acid in the recovery process.

(6 marks)

Total: 6 marks

■ ■ ■

Candidates' answers to Question 4

Candidate A

Lactic acid reduces the pH of the muscle cells, which inhibits the action of enzymes in the cells. The build-up of lactic acid causes discomfort and pain. As enzyme action is inhibited, important reactions cannot take place to yield energy. This causes fatigue and, therefore, a decrease in the overall work of the muscle. In the recovery process, an increased amount of oxygen is provided by EPOC (excess post-exercise oxygen consumption). This, along with sub-maximal exercise, helps to remove the lactic acid. Lactic acid is mainly removed in sweat and in urine. Small amounts are exhaled. A very small amount of lactic acid is used to resynthesise adenosine triphosphate (ATP).

Candidate B

Lactic acid is produced when the exercise level is at a high intensity. This level is referred to as the anaerobic phase, when the body is producing energy without oxygen.

The production of lactic acid inhibits muscle action, so the performer cannot produce maximum effort in the affected muscles. This period of intense exercise also creates an oxygen debt and EPOC becomes part of the recovery process. EPOC has two components: alactacid, which helps replenish the oxygen, and lactacid, which gets rid of the waste products, one of which is lactic acid.

The effects of lactic acid on the body include an increased rate of breathing, muscle soreness and a feeling of fatigue. All this is because of the build-up of lactic acid in the body.

🖉 Both candidates make a good attempt at answering this question, but do so in different styles. Candidate A produces a thorough answer but puts it all in one paragraph. Candidate B breaks the answer into smaller chunks, which is easier to follow. However, Candidate B fails to answer all parts of the question fully by not commenting on the fate of lactic acid in the recovery process and only scores 3 marks. Candidate A covers this in the last point and scores the maximum 6 marks.

The ATP–PC system

The ATP–PC system is one of three ways the body resynthesises ATP.

(a) Describe the intensity and duration of a sporting activity in which phosphocreatine is the predominant fuel source. (3 marks)

(b) Discuss the advantages and disadvantages of using phosphocreatine as a fuel. (2 marks)

Total: 5 marks

■ ■ ■

Candidates' answers to Question 5

Candidate A

(a) The phosphocreatine system provides the bulk of ATP during explosive or powerful sports actions, such as a shot putter or a sprinter pushing off from the blocks.

(b) Advantages and disadvantages of using phosphocreatine as a fuel are outlined in the table below.

Advantages	Disadvantages
Creates maximal power for 10 seconds	Can take 5–7 minutes to replenish PC store
PC is a simple compound that is easy to break down	This energy store doesn't last too long

Candidate B

(a) The PC system creates energy in the following way:

$$Pc \longrightarrow P + CREATINE + energy$$

It produces energy which is used in fast and powerful movements. The stores of PC held in the body can produce maximum effort for only about 10 seconds. The PC system does not rely on the presence of oxygen and is therefore referred to as an anaerobic form of energy production.

(b) The advantage of the energy produced by the PC system is that because it does not rely on the presence of oxygen, it can happen very quickly. This reaction does not produce any harmful waste products which could limit performance. There are no disadvantages with this system.

✒ There is a contrast in the way the candidates have answered part (a); the key words in the question are intensity and duration. Candidate A manages to refer to these in short answers and also makes links to named sporting examples and therefore scores the maximum 3 marks. Candidate B does give a technical explanation, and makes points relating to time (10 seconds), but is a little vague with the term 'powerful and fast' — these could also be applied to other energy systems. No reference is made to a sporting activity in the answer. Candidate B would only score 1 mark. In part (b), again there is a contrast in styles. Candidate A puts the answer into a table which is clear to follow and can be used in the exam as long as the text within each block makes sense. One mark each is available for an advantage and a disadvantage and this answer gains the maximum 2. More than one answer has been given and this is good exam technique. Candidate B makes a good point about the waste products but does not give a disadvantage and would only score 1 mark for this section. Candidate A scores the maximum 5 marks for this question while Candidate B only scores 2 marks.

DOMS

High-intensity training may be followed by DOMS.
(a) Explain the term 'DOMS', outlining both its causes and effects. (5 marks)
(b) Outline the precautions that an athlete can undertake in order to try to minimise DOMS. (3 marks)

Total: 8 marks

■ ■ ■

Candidates' answers to Question 6

Candidate A

(a) DOMS stands for 'delayed onset of muscle soreness'. It usually occurs 24–48 hours after intense exercise or a sports competition such as a football match.

It results from damaged muscle fibres and may have been caused by poor preparation, such as not warming up properly. Performers may experience DOMS when they try a new exercise or training method.

(b) Athletes can try to prevent DOMS by preparing for training or competition in the correct manner. This includes doing a proper warm-up that targets all the muscle groups that will be used and making sure that they cool down properly at the end of the session. In order to help repair damage to muscle fibres, the England rugby team get into an ice bath. This also helps reduce the chance of DOMS.

Candidate B

(a) ● DOMS = delayed onset of muscle soreness.
● Effect — micro damage to muscle fibres, which causes inflammation. This causes pain.
● Cause — intensive exercise.
● The athlete has pushed himself or herself to the point of overload.
● It is often caused by eccentric contraction, such as when running downhill.
● It can also occur when an athlete starts training after a period of rest, or tries a new method of training.

(b) DOMS can be prevented by ensuring that an athlete undertakes a thorough warm-up and also ends each session with a thorough cool-down.

Candidate A produces a good answer to both parts of the question. The candidate clearly has an understanding of the concept of DOMS and makes good reference to sporting examples. However, not enough points are made in (a) to score full marks. Candidate A scores 4 of the available 5 marks in (a) and gains the maximum 3 marks in (b), for a detailed answer. Candidate B sets out the answer to (a) clearly. It is easy to follow and covers all the parts of the question. The format used makes it easy for both the candidate and the examiner to check that all parts of the question are answered. Candidate B scores the maximum 5 marks for (a), but drops a mark in (b) by failing to make enough points to match the marks available. Overall, both candidates score 7 marks.

Sporting ability and the environment

To what extent is the development of sports ability affected by the environment. (50 marks)

Total: 50 marks

■ ■ ■

Candidates' answers to Question 7

Candidate A

In answering the question, I will cover the following points. First, I will define the key terms and then give a brief overview of the topic area, focusing on individual differences and their effect on access to sport. Using examples from a range of global games, I will identify how different cultures are more suited to particular sports. In conclusion, I will review the current situation and suggest where this sports issue may be in the next century, giving my opinions on the effects of the environment on sportspeople today.

The keywords I will be discussing include 'physiological', which refers to physical components. In my answer, I will focus on the body's adaptation to the environment in which it is trained. Another key term is 'psychological', which refers to the way the mind works and perceives information. 'Mechanical issues' in sport involve movement, analysis and correct preparation for performance. The term 'sociocultural' refers to a person's social and cultural background. 'Innate' refers to what is inherited — natural traits passed down from our parents. 'Nurture' refers to a person's upbringing and social background.

Before advances in sports technology, it was only the naturally talented sportspeople who would be noticed in sport because those people who had not inherited skills and specific physiological advantages did not have the chances to improve like athletes have in global games today.

Basketball players exemplify a stereotypical sporting body type. The body shape of a basketball player is typically ectomorphic–mesomorphic. Somatotype is an innate feature that can affect an athlete's performance. An example of how the cultural environment can affect sporting pathways is seen in black basketball players. Many black Americans are brought up in similar sociocultural conditions — in lower class ghettoes that have many basketball courts. Therefore, in high school, it is often expected that young black males will be interested in basketball. This idea is referred to as a self-fulfilling prophecy.

Certain groups have sporting opportunities affected by the society in which they live. An example would be female athletes — due to a lack of self-esteem. The collapse of several female athletes in the 1928 Olympic 800 metres track event resulted in it being banned until 1964.

Sports ability can be developed from any level. An athlete who is already trained to a high level may undergo less adaptation and development than an untrained athlete.

However, since we can all potentially change aspects of our bodies, such as VO_2max and our muscle fibres by around 15% from our natural state, then it could be argued that the environment and the way we train are the only things that affect sports development because we cannot change what is innate to us. People who come from naturally sporting families will have an initial advantage. For example, they could have naturally higher VO_2max values or be able to delay the threshold of each energy system for longer.

Given the right facilities, coaching and access, the fitness of people who do not have a naturally high fitness level can be improved dramatically. This is where sociocultural and economic aspects play a part in the development of a sportsperson. The same can be said for innately talented sportspeople — unless they have opportunities to improve their fitness, then it won't improve.

In sports that require only limited facilities and money, all types of people from different backgrounds can participate and reach a level of excellence. A good example of this is the London marathon. In long-distance running many of the best athletes are Kenyan. They have an innate advantage because they come from an environment that is at altitude. Therefore, they are born to cope with a low-oxygen atmosphere, which gives them an advantage in aerobic events such as the marathon.

However, athletes who were not born at altitude, such as Paula Radcliffe, still compete and win marathons. This is due to expert training and facilities. Many athletes also use technology to try to compensate for genetic difference. For example, athletes in the west use hypoxic chambers to try to create the same conditions of living and training at altitude. So, the chances of success of Radcliffe, who was born with some ability and the physiology needed to be a marathon runner, are greatly affected by the environment in which she lives and trains.

The environment has many psychological influences that affect our attitudes towards sport. The stereotypical sportsperson is outgoing, conscientious and courageous. These traits could be inherited from parents, but they could also be the result of influences from the environment in which the individual was brought up. Attitudes and beliefs often develop when a great deal of time is spent within a particular environment. For example, someone with a passion for sport is likely to attend a sporting university, which would be very competitive. Such an environment could change even the most introverted people.

The environment in which people live affects the sports they take up and also the progress that they achieve. In Kenya, children see long-distance runners as role models. The idea of self-fulfilling prophecy comes into play here, as they feel that this is the only sporting path open to them.

In conclusion, the environment of sport plays a big role in the development of sports ability. Physiological and psychological components can be changed through training methods and are affected by sociocultural and economic backgrounds. I think that although we have stable traits, the situation we are in can affect personalities and attitudes in sport. Also, inherited physiological components give some people a major advantage. However, without the opportunity to maintain or improve their levels of fitness, such people may continue to be only average competitors. So, children should be encouraged into sport, because even if they are not the best to start with, they will have the opportunity to become the best they can be.

Candidate B

The question is all about the debate on nature v nurture and I will use examples from a range of global sports to develop this. Ability in sport refers to the ideas sports psychologists have developed which suggest that these are the basic foundations that help us to learn sports skills. Some psychologists argue that most of the abilities are inherited or innate. This is the so-called nature debate. Others argue that these abilities are affected by the environment and the experiences we go through; this is referred to as the nurture debate. The question also relates to the debate on whether the environment affects ability in sport.

Most teams, when they are preparing for major competitions, spend time acclimatising to the environmental conditions they will experience in the finals. Before the 2004 Olympic Games, the British team spent time in a training camp in Cyprus. This was an attempt to get used to the temperature and climate they could expect in Athens. This would suggest that elite sports people believe that their ability can be affected by the environment. However, I am talking about elite athletes with a high level of talent and so the environment may not affect their skill too much.

France has developed a high altitude training centre in the Pyrenees called Font Romeu, which enables the French national teams and international athletes to prepare within their own country for global competitions at altitude. This benefits sports that have a heavy aerobic element; the main advantage is that the athletes do not have to leave their own country during their preparation phase.

In sports such as long distance running there is evidence, both scientific and in terms of records and championships, that athletes who compete in longer distance events have a distinct advantage if they are born or train within areas of high altitude. The East African Rift Valley in Kenya has produced many great runners and there is little doubt that the high altitude environment in which they live plays an important part in their high level of skill and success in these events.

Abilities are mainly innate, enduring characteristics; the most important in sport appear to be psychomotor and gross motor abilities. Many argue that unless you are born with these abilities you will not make good progress in your chosen sport. This tends to play down the effect of the environment. For example, elite tennis players competing in the international grand slam tournaments have a high level of innate ability, which means they can compete at a very high level in all types of environments. However, players such as Tim Henman are said to favour a particular surface (in his case grass), which does depend on the environment.

In some countries such as the former East Germany and Australia, they have attempted to identify this innate ability in young people as early as possible, taking them into institutes of sport where the environment is controlled to give them more chance of achieving excellence in sport; this process combines both the nature and nurture approach. In both cases this approach has been successful and suggests that a combination of both approaches is best. Bringing all the best performers together creates an atmosphere of excellence that helps all athletes develop their ability in sport. This is especially true where athletes use technology and biomechanics to enhance their performance. Very often the role of the scientists based in these institutes is to simulate the effects of nature, such as creating high altitude environments in hypoxic chambers where athletes can train. The usual adaptations from altitude training can be achieved, but without the athlete actually having to go to a specific geographical area.

Therefore, in conclusion, I have shown that there are many such cases where ability can be affected by the environment. However, there is a counter-argument that suggests an athlete's innate ability is still the deciding factor in the acquisition of skill. In truth, the answer probably lies somewhere between the two and I am sure that scientists and sports specialists will continue to research and argue over this. An elite athlete should pay attention to both sides of the debate; practice makes perfect, training in the right environment and working on and developing skills can only improve performance at the global level.

e This question requires candidates to develop the argument of nature versus nurture. Candidate A manages to develop such an argument. The answer has a sound structure and moves along well, with both introductory and concluding paragraphs. The candidate includes some practical examples, but these need to be developed further. The candidate has clearly worked on an essay style and stuck to it. However, this does not always relate directly to the question. Candidate A scores 27 of the 50 marks available. Candidate B identifies the key debate and presents the answer in a slightly different, more direct, style. The answer includes more terminology and brings in a range of scientific points. Candidate B scores 38 out of 50 marks.

Technology in the preparation of elite athletes

Discuss how technology can be used by elite athletes preparing for global competition:

(50 marks)

Total: 50 marks

■ ■ ■

Candidates' answers to Question 8

Candidate A

In this essay I will first define the following key terms and phrases: technology, ergogenic aids and preparation. Using examples, I will discuss the role of modern technology before, during and after an event. Preparation for a global sports event can be in the short term, for example 48 hours before competition, or long-term — 7 weeks or longer before the event. Both short- and long-term factors need to be considered, so that correct training, nutrition and rest can be prescribed. In an attempt to build up the athlete's confidence, preparation could involve an evaluation from a previous competition, outlining strengths and weaknesses. Many athletes use advances in technology to improve their performance. They may use ergogenic aids. An ergogenic aid is any factor that enhances performance, such as the hypoxic chamber in which David Beckham slept to keep his VO_2max high, after he had broken his foot and was unable to train. Heart monitors are becoming increasingly widespread, even in amateur training. They are a quick and easy way to check the level of your training. In addition, they can be used in most sports, even swimming.

With increased knowledge, education and funding, technology has advanced rapidly. There has recently been a claim that football shirts will be fitted with sensors to monitor heart rate, sweating and breathing. The sensors will be linked to a computer that will process the player's level of fatigue.

The role of technology is to analyse training, and to enhance and evaluate performance. This can have many positive effects on an athlete's preparation for a competition. For example, a swimmer preparing for a World Championship may prepare by videoing his or her dives from recent competitions and training sessions, and then, along with an expert in biomechanics and a computer, analyse what can be done to achieve greater distance from the dive. This type of feedback is extrinsic and can only be given at the end of the performance, so that the swimmer gains a fuller understanding. This is especially true of swimming, because the remarks of the coach cannot be heard in a training or race situation.

Heart rate monitors can be used to check the intensity of the training. In the case of swimmers, waterproof watches and wetboards can be used to record times and compare personal bests. Wearing body suits can enhance the performance of

swimmers. It is claimed that less water sticks to a full body costume called a 'skin', thus making the body more streamlined in the water.

Not only can technology enhance performance, it can — and has been increasingly used to — speed up recovery from injuries. The Alba machine, costing £65 000, helped Roy Keane play in an important match only 22 days after tearing a hamstring.

Although technology has many benefits, its misuse can lead to cheating and deviance in sport. Peer pressure and the desire to be first (with the huge extrinsic rewards this brings) often push athletes to try to gain unfair advantage. The most common way they do this is by taking drugs. Steroids, for example, are used to gain muscle bulk.

Training schedules are so busy during the lead up to a competition that athletes are given narcotic analgesics (pain killers) to help them cope with the pain and the strain on their bodies.

In the Olympic games held in Athens, Greece 2004, during the women's backstroke heats, British swimmer Sarah Price hit an underwater camera and cut her leg. She was in pain and unable to swim in the 200 m event. This ruined her chances of a place in the final and destroyed all the hard work and preparation she had put in previously. Therefore, technology may not always have a positive effect and sometimes a performance may be affected by its use.

In my opinion, though, technology and science have many benefits in enhancing training and improving understanding. However, when drugs are used the sport is no longer sport. It becomes a battle of which team has the most money to buy the best equipment and employ the best coaches and sports scientists.

Candidate B

'Faster, higher, stronger' is the motto of the Olympic movement. However, in the twenty-first century a better motto might be 'bigger, heavier, taller'. This could be because of modern technology and the role it plays in the analysis, enhancement and evaluation of performance.

In attempting to answer the question, I will cover the following points. After defining the key terms, I will give a brief overview of the types of technology that can be used in preparation by global athletes. Using examples from a range of global games, I will identify the reasons for the apparent rise in the use of technology during preparation. To conclude, I will review the current use of technology in sport, outline where I think the issue may go in the future and give my personal opinion.

The use of technology in sport is not new. However, today, technology in sport is exploited. Athletes can use it to enhance their performance and in some cases they are guilty of deviance.

Ergogenic aids are those substances or technical aids that enhance sporting performance. Some, such as special clothing, are classed as legal. For example, in the Sydney Olympics in 2000, gold medallist Cathy Freeman wore a full body suit. The suit, named the 'swift suit', was made by Nike and was designed to be light, breathable, cause less friction and, most importantly, faster. Other ergogenic aids, such as drugs, are illegal. However, they are widely used in sport. An example of this is the case of Olympic sprinter Ben Johnson, who was banned from competition for taking drugs to enhance his performance. Taking drugs defeats the object of sportsmanship.

Technology has improved in sport, leading to better performances across a wide range of sports. Preparation carried out by athletes is helped by better systems, such as the equipment used to measure heart rate. By measuring and recording heart rate at different points in their performance, athletes can work out their aerobic and anaerobic thresholds and use this information to set training zones.

The use of science in both nutrition and mental preparation has increased, allowing dietitians to work out suitable diets for athletes and sports psychologists to work with athletes to keep them motivated and positive.

Over the last 10 years, there has also been a dramatic increase in technology in terms of sports clothing. In football, 'smart shirts' have been trialled by Arsenal FC. These shirts detect the players' heart rates and levels of sweating. This information is sent to a computer in the dugout, letting the coaches know if any players are fatigued.

Technology can be used to analyse training during the preparation of an athlete. Whilst training, there can be internal monitoring of heart rate, blood lactate and brain activity, and also external monitoring such as video recording. This was used by Cathy Freeman, so that physiologists could study the 3-dimensional video and work out the most important biomechanical parameters of her running technique. This enables athletes to correct errors.

Technology can be used in training to enhance performance. An example of such technology is the hypoxic chamber. This is like a tent that can be slept in to improve an athlete's aerobic capacity. It was designed as a substitute for altitude training. David Beckham used a hypoxic chamber in preparation for the 2002 football World Cup finals. After breaking his toe, he slept in an oxygen-deficient atmosphere in order to maintain his aerobic capacity. He did gain match fitness. This is an example of technology not being fully developed, as it cannot yet be used to speed up the repair of broken bones. In threshold training, technology can be used to detect an athlete's energy thresholds. Therefore, the onset of blood lactate (OBLA) can be detected and training can be adjusted to delay this.

Technology can be used in the evaluation of performance. Video analysis of technique is used during this part of the preparation for an event. A digital video review system is now in operation at Leicester RUFC. Costing £40 000, the system enables coaching staff to review images while a game is in progress in order to pinpoint opposition weaknesses.

I believe that technology, because of Americanisation, will continue to grow in sport. Technology can enhance performance, help prevent injuries and speed up recovery. An example of this is a laser treatment that heats up damaged muscles, increasing the speed of blood flow and, therefore, speeding up recovery. Roy Keane tore a hamstring but was back playing within 22 days. This type of injury would normally take 6 weeks to heal.

This essay has been about the advantages of technology. However, there are disadvantages, including the increased use of drugs in sport. This problem is being slowly overcome because of improved technology in drug detection. There is also the case that sport is becoming more mechanistic and less entertaining.

e This question requires candidates to discuss the role that technology plays in the preparation of athletes for global competition. Both candidates make good attempts at answering the question, but their examples are rather limited. Candidate A makes a number of valid points and does bring in some scientific facts from different units. The examples used are a little vague and mostly relate to sport in the UK. Remember, the focus for answers in the synoptic section should relate to a range of global sports competitions. This essay just about answers the question and scores 29 marks out of the possible 50. Candidate B gives a wider range of examples, and these do come from the different scientific topic areas of Unit 6. The candidate makes a good range of points and uses technical terms. However, at times the points are not fully explained. Candidate B starts to analyse the issue and, towards the end, develops a counter-argument. It is a pity that this ends rather abruptly. The answer would benefit from a fuller conclusion. Overall, this is a good attempt, worth 36 marks.

Long-term planning

Long-term planning is important in the preparation of elite athletes for global competition.

Explain the various factors that elite athletes need to consider when planning long term. (50 marks)

Total: 50 marks

■ ■ ■

Candidates' answers to Question 9

Candidate A

This question refers to the macro-cycle of an athlete's planning. I will attempt to discuss and explain the main factors that a footballer preparing for a new season would consider. Most athletes break up their training programmes into three main phases: the macro-cycle, which can last for up to 6 months; the meso-cycle which is usually around 4–6 weeks — long enough to enable the longest-term adaptations to occur; and the micro-cycle — the athlete's weekly plan, showing a balance between training and rest. Also, there may be a competition.

For footballers, and others in team sports, many of these decisions are taken by a manager or coach, working with individual athletes. There may be factors relating to the team that need to be taken into consideration. For example, footballers playing for Chelsea, a team looking to do well in both national and European competitions, may need to plan to fit in with the squad system used. It is possible that they may not play every week, thus releasing time to work on specific fitness or skill requirements.

When footballers return to training at the start of what is referred to as the close season, they often start by doing a series of fitness tests to work out their starting positions. This is a factor that must be taken into consideration. Players need to set themselves targets for their fitness over the season. Some players may be recovering from injury — for example, when Wayne Rooney started playing again after being injured in the European finals. Such players may need to set themselves a target for when they think they will be able to start full-time training again.

When players set goals and targets they should follow the SMARTER principle. This refers to targets that are specific to individual players. This could involve working on a specific 'S' aspect of fitness, such as improving their speed over 30 metres. The goals need to be measurable 'M', so that they can be worked towards — for example, setting a time to beat. 'A' stands for achievable. In terms of this question it means something to be achieved by the end of the season. For example, they could set themselves the target of scoring 20 goals in the season. 'R' stands for recorded. This could be a tally of the goals scored or their speed over 30 metres. 'T' is for timed. They could give themselves checkmarks throughout the season, for example to have scored 11 goals by Christmas. 'E' and 'R' stand for effective and reviewed, which could be something for players to work out with their coach to ensure targets improve performance. This could be reviewed on a regular basis.

These are the many factors that an athlete needs to take into account during long-term preparation.

Candidate B

I will try to answer the question set by referring to British athletes preparing for the Olympic Games in Athens. The Olympic Games tend to be held in the August of an Olympic year. This gives athletes a clear goal to plan towards. I will suggest the main factors that should be considered in long-term planning and conclude by giving my own opinion.

Preparing for major global games often includes periods of acclimatisation. This means getting used to the type of climate and environment that will be experienced during the games. Very often, international teams, such as the Great Britain Olympic team, prepare for major events by setting up training camps in an attempt to allow the performers to acclimatise. In preparation for the Athens games, the British team set up a training camp for a year in Cyprus. This ensured that the athletes trained in conditions similar to those in Athens.

If the event is to be at altitude, then the athletes need to simulate this in their training. At altitude there is less oxygen in the air, so the athletes have to work harder. Altitude training can be used to maximise aerobic capacity. Technology has been developed that can be used to simulate altitude. Institutes of sport, such as the AIS, have special rooms (hypoxic chambers) in which the amount of oxygen can be controlled, thus replicating the type of environment in which the athletes will compete.

Training camps are also important in helping to develop team spirit and teamwork. This can have an important impact on the psychology of the team and help give the team confidence. Recently, it was reported in the press that the British Lions rugby team had already met for a weekend to try to develop this type of team bonding before the tour of New Zealand.

Competing for a country involves national pride, which can sometimes make teams nervous. It is important that the stress levels of the team are considered when planning for competitions. Many teams use sports psychologists to help them prepare. Psychologists might start working with the team up to a year before the competition. A BBC television programme reported on the work a sports psychologist had been doing with the Scottish women's bowls team as they prepared for the last Commonwealth Games. The team members were nervous about playing at a big competition. However, they learned how to use relaxation techniques and went on to win the gold medal.

> This is quite an open question that allows candidates to answer using a range of examples and points from across the scientific units. Candidate A focuses on one specific sport in the UK. This does work in a limited way, but the examples are restricted. Always try to include examples from a range of global games. Candidate A makes some original and valid points from Unit 3, 6(a) and 6(b). However, there is not much structure to the answer and some of the paragraphs are rather long. Candidate B

makes a range of key points and develops an original answer. The examples used are from a range of sports and are contemporary. There is evidence that the candidate has been reading reports in newspapers — always a good idea. The candidate also makes, and attempts to explain, some points from a range of scientific areas. However, the essay is not well structured. Indeed, both candidates' essays would benefit from concluding paragraphs. Candidate A scores 27 of the available 50 marks. Candidate B makes a wider range of points and uses global examples, earning the higher score of 35 marks.

Short-term preparation

Short-term preparation for elite competition can involve physiological, psychological and mechanical considerations.

Using examples from sports you have studied, discuss how elite athletes spend the last 48 hours before competition. (50 marks)

Total: 50 marks

■ ■ ■

Candidates' answers to Question 10

Candidate A

The final 48 hours before an elite competition are all about psyching up the athletes and preparing them mentally for the competition. In some sports, for example rugby and football, teams meet up in a hotel or training centre 2 days before a major event, such as a World Cup match. This means that the manager or coach can spend the maximum time getting the players mentally ready for the competition.

The England football team has team meetings during the last few days, with only light training. They might work on set piece moves, such as free kicks and corners. The meetings can also be useful in helping the team to bond. This could be particularly important if it is some time since they played together as a team.

Some teams, for example the British Lions rugby team, do tasks together in order to help build team spirit. The Lions team is made up of players from different countries, so it is important that they learn to pull together and play as a team as soon as possible.

Team meetings that take place the day before the competition can be used to go over the tactics to be used in the game. The players might watch videos of the team they are going to play against. In football, goalkeepers (e.g. David James) study the opposing team's penalty-takers to help them decide which way to dive. This is particularly important if the game has to be decided on penalties.

Closer to the game, the players need to understand the theory behind the inverted-U hypothesis of Yerkes and Dodson. This is the idea of an optimum zone of arousal in which an athlete is in the perfect mental state to play his or her sport. For some players, this may mean having to motivate themselves — players sometimes use music or self-talk to get themselves into the zone. Others may be over-aroused and have to relax to get back into the zone. This could be done using learned relaxation techniques; again players may use music to help with their nerves. If the game were, say, a World Cup final, then most of the players would be very nervous and the manager or coach would need to raise their confidence, getting them to focus on the game itself and specific jobs that they need to do. It is always difficult when a coach is dealing with a team because players will have different levels of arousal.

In the last few hours before competition, players will be narrowing down their attention. This is called selective attention — concentrating on the important cues that they will get from the game. At this point, the team will be together in private, usually in the changing rooms, in an attempt to cut out all distractions. Shortly before kick off they will go out and warm up on the pitch. This will also help them to prepare mentally for the game by taking in the atmosphere and getting used to the crowd.

By following the above routine, the players should be fully prepared for their competition and should be able to compete at a high level. The key is to make sure each player is in the optimum zone when they begin playing. Coaches and managers use the last 48 hours before a game to try to achieve this.

Candidate B

There are numerous factors that elite athletes need to consider in their final preparations for a global competition. I will explain the physiological, psychological and mechanical considerations using, as a case study, the England football team preparing for a World Cup qualifying match.

Usually a national team will meet up a couple of days before an important match. The England football team often uses Bisham Abbey — one of the UK sports institutes. This provides a training base where they can prepare physiologically and practise strategies and tactics. Bisham Abbey also has rooms and areas where the team can meet and talk through the game. The manager, Sven Goran Eriksson, may want to explain a particular way he wants the team to play, so this would bring in some psychological considerations.

In terms of physiology, the players' training and level of work should taper down as the match approaches. The final 18 hours should involve resting. This should ensure full energy stores — in particular, glycogen stores. The players can help this by carbohydrate loading in the last 48 hours. This means eating a diet containing at least 70% complex carbohydrates, such as pasta. This will maximise glycogen stores in both the muscles and the liver. Players also need to increase their fluid intake before the game, because a 1% drop in hydration levels can lead to a 10% drop in performance. Players often use isotonic drinks.

In terms of psychological factors, the key is that players need to be in the right mental state as they prepare for the match. They need to psych themselves up. This should not be too difficult for professional sportsmen playing for their country because such people mostly have a 'need to achieve' or 'NACH' drive in their personalities. Players might be nervous. This can affect different people in different ways. Many international teams now use sports psychologists to help players prepare mentally for games. This could involve using imagery, for example getting players to focus on key parts of the game or to watch themselves playing in successful matches. The night before the game the players have a team meeting during which instructions are given and key points made.

Mechanical considerations could include matching the playing kit and boots to the likely conditions. If it is going to be wet and cold, players will want long-sleeved shirts and possibly gloves. They will also need longer studs in their boots. There is a limit

to the factors that can be changed mechanically in such a short time period — players could work on basic skills on the morning of the game. Analysis will be carried out after the game. Players and coaches will study videos and use computer programmes such as 'prozone', which tracks the movement and involvement of each player.

In the last few hours before the game, the main focus is on warming up properly. This is to ensure that the body is in the best possible state before competing. The warm-up may well start some hours before the game. Often the players do some light exercise and stretching at the hotel before leaving to go to the stadium. At the stadium, there are two further warm-up sessions, one of which is on the pitch about 30 minutes before kick off. This gives players a chance to get a feel for the conditions and also to make adjustments to kit. This can also help with their mental and psychological preparation, helping to settle any pre-match nerves. The final warm-up and team talk take place in the changing rooms. In big stadia, such as the Millennium Stadium in Cardiff, there are warm-up areas next to the changing rooms. This allows players to finally stretch and prepare for their game.

✍ This question requires candidates to discuss the physiological, psychological and mechanical aspects of short-term preparation. Candidate A produces a reasonable answer with a number of relevant examples. However, only those points relating to psychological factors are developed. Therefore, the candidate has only partly answered the question set. This is an important point and one that unfortunately many candidates fail to grasp — you *must* answer the question as it is set. Unfortunately, Candidate A's answer only scores 18 of the 50 marks available. Candidate B answers the question in a more direct and structured way. The candidate works through all parts of the question, bringing in a range of subject areas. The use of one case study works well, although the answer could have been expanded with reference to other sports and global competitions. The essay also ends rather abruptly and would have benefited from introductory and concluding paragraphs. However, Candidate B has answered the question set and scores 30 marks.